On this Day - February 14th

By

Kerry Butters.

February 14 is the 45th day of the year in the Gregorian calendar. There are 320 days remaining until the end of the year (321 in leap years). This date is slightly more likely to fall on a Tuesday, Thursday or Sunday (58 in 400 years each) than on Friday or Saturday (57), and slightly less likely to occur on a Monday or Wednesday (56).

Contents

February 14th

Events

- 748 – Abbasid Revolution: The Hashimi rebels under Abu Muslim Khorasani take Merv, capital of the Umayyad province Khorasan, marking the consolidation of the Abbasid revolt.
- 842 – Charles the Bald and Louis the German swear the Oaths of Strasbourg in the French and German languages.
- 1014 – Pope Benedict VIII crowns Henry of Bavaria, King of Germany and of Italy, as Holy Roman Emperor.
- 1076 – Pope Gregory VII excommunicates Henry IV, Holy Roman Emperor.
- 1130 – Pope Innocent II is elected.

- 1349 – Several hundred Jews are burned to death by mobs while the remaining Jews are forcibly removed from Strasbourg.
- 1400 – Richard II of England dies, most probably from starvation, in Pontefract Castle, on the orders of Henry Bolingbroke.
- 1502 – Spanish Inquisition: The Catholic Monarchs issue a decree forcing Muslims in Granada to convert to Catholicism or leave Spain.
- 1530 – Spanish conquistadores, led by Nuño de Guzmán, overthrow and execute Tangaxuan II, the last independent monarch of the Tarascan state in present-day central Mexico.
- 1556 – Thomas Cranmer is declared a heretic.
- 1655 – Arauco War: The Mapuche under their elected military leader, Clentaru, rise up against the Spanish in an insurrection in present-day central Chile.
- 1778 – The United States flag is formally recognized by a foreign naval vessel for the first time, when French Admiral Toussaint-Guillaume Picquet de la Motte renders a nine gun salute to USS *Ranger*, commanded by John Paul Jones.
- 1779 – American Revolutionary War: The Battle of Kettle Creek is fought in Georgia.
- 1779 – James Cook is killed by Native Hawaiians near Kealakekua on the Island of Hawaii.
- 1797 – French Revolutionary Wars: Battle of Cape St. Vincent: John Jervis, (later 1st Earl of St Vincent)

and Horatio Nelson (later 1st Viscount Nelson) lead the British Royal Navy to victory over a Spanish fleet in action near Gibraltar.

- 1804 – Karađorđe leads the First Serbian Uprising against the Ottoman Empire.
- 1831 – Ras Marye of Yejju marches into Tigray and defeats and kills Dejazmach Sabagadis in the Battle of Debre Abbay.
- 1835 – The original Quorum of the Twelve Apostles, in the Latter Day Saint movement, is formed in Kirtland, Ohio.
- 1849 – In New York City, James Knox Polk becomes the first serving President of the United States to have his photograph taken.
- 1852 – Great Ormond St Hospital for Sick Children, the first hospital in England to provide in-patient beds specifically for children, is founded in London.
- 1855 – Texas is linked by telegraph to the rest of the United States, with the completion of a connection between New Orleans and Marshall, Texas.
- 1859 – Oregon is admitted as the 33rd U.S. state.
- 1876 – Alexander Graham Bell applies for a patent for the telephone, as does Elisha Gray.
- 1879 – The War of the Pacific breaks out when Chilean armed forces occupy the Bolivian port city of Antofagasta.
- 1899 – Voting machines are approved by the U.S. Congress for use in federal elections.

- 1900 – British forces begin the Battle of the Tugela Heights in an effort to lift the Siege of Ladysmith.
- 1903 – The United States Department of Commerce and Labor is established (later split into the Department of Commerce and the Department of Labor).
- 1912 – Arizona is admitted as the 48th U.S. state.
- 1912 – In Groton, Connecticut, the first diesel-powered submarine is commissioned.
- 1918 – The Soviet Union adopts the Gregorian calendar (on 1 February according to the Julian calendar).
- 1919 – The Polish–Soviet War begins.
- 1920 – The League of Women Voters is founded in Chicago.
- 1924 – The Computing-Tabulating-Recording Company changes its name to International Business Machines Corporation (IBM).
- 1929 – Saint Valentine's Day Massacre: Seven people, six of them gangster rivals of Al Capone's gang, are murdered in Chicago.
- 1942 – Battle of Pasir Panjang contributes to the fall of Singapore.
- 1943 – World War II: Rostov-on-Don, Russia is liberated.
- 1943 – World War II: Tunisia Campaign: General Hans-Jürgen von Arnim's Fifth Panzer Army launches a concerted attack against Allied positions in Tunisia.

- 1944 – World War II: In the Action of 14 February 1944, a British submarine sinks a German-controlled Italian submarine in the Strait of Malacca.
- 1945 – World War II: On the first day of the bombing of Dresden, the British Royal Air Force and the United States Army Air Forces begin fire-bombing Dresden.
- 1945 – World War II: Navigational error leads to the mistaken bombing of Prague, Czechoslovakia by an American squadron of B-17s assisting in the Soviet's Vistula–Oder Offensive.
- 1945 – World War II: Mostar is liberated by Yugoslav partisans
- 1945 – President Franklin D. Roosevelt meets with King Ibn Saud of Saudi Arabia aboard the USS *Quincy*, officially beginning U.S.-Saudi diplomatic relations.
- 1946 – The Bank of England is nationalized.
- 1949 – The Knesset (Israeli parliament) convenes for the first time.
- 1949 – The Asbestos Strike begins in Canada. The strike marks the beginning of the Quiet Revolution in Quebec.
- 1950 – Chinese Civil War: The National Revolutionary Army instigates the unsuccessful Battle of Tianquan against the People's Liberation Army.
- 1956 – The 20th Congress of the Communist Party of the Soviet Union begins in Moscow. On the last night

of the meeting, Premier Nikita Khrushchev condemns Joseph Stalin's crimes in a secret speech.

- 1961 – Discovery of the chemical elements: Element 103, Lawrencium, is first synthesized at the University of California.
- 1962 – First Lady Jacqueline Kennedy takes television viewers on a tour of the White House.
- 1966 – Australian currency is decimalised.
- 1970 – The iconic live album *Live at Leeds* by The Who is recorded.
- 1979 – In Kabul, Setami Milli militants kidnap the American ambassador to Afghanistan, Adolph Dubs who is later killed during a gunfight between his kidnappers and police.
- 1981 – Stardust fire: A fire in a Dublin nightclub kills 48 people
- 1983 – United American Bank of Knoxville, Tennessee collapses. Its president, Jake Butcher, is later convicted of fraud.
- 1989 – Union Carbide agrees to pay $470 million to the Indian government for damages it caused in the 1984 Bhopal disaster.
- 1989 – Iranian leader Ruhollah Khomeini issues a fatwa encouraging Muslims to kill Salman Rushdie, author of *The Satanic Verses*.
- 1990 – Ninety-two people are killed when Indian Airlines Flight 605 crashes in Bangalore, India.

- 1990 – The *Voyager 1* spacecraft takes the photograph of planet Earth later become famous as *Pale Blue Dot*.
- 1998 – An oil tanker train collides with a freight train in Yaoundé, Cameroon, spilling fuel oil. One person scavenging the oil created a massive explosion which kills 120.
- 2000 – The spacecraft *NEAR Shoemaker* enters orbit around asteroid 433 Eros, the first spacecraft to orbit an asteroid.
- 2004 – In a suburb of Moscow, Russia, the roof of the Transvaal water park collapses, killing more than 25 people, and wounding more than 100 others.
- 2005 – Lebanese self-made billionaire and business tycoon Rafic Hariri is killed, along with 21 others, when explosives, equivalent of around 1,000 kg of TNT, are detonated as his motorcade drove near the St. George Hotel in Beirut.
- 2005 – Seven people are killed and 151 wounded in a series of bombings by suspected al-Qaeda-linked militants that hit the Philippines' Makati financial district in Metro Manila, Davao City, and General Santos City.
- 2005 – YouTube is launched by a group of college students, eventually becoming the largest video sharing website in the world and a main source for viral videos.
- 2008 – Northern Illinois University shooting: A gunman opened fire in a lecture hall of the DeKalb

County, Illinois university resulting in six fatalities (including gunman) and 21 injuries.

- 2011 – As a part of Arab Spring, the Bahraini uprising, a series of demonstrations, amounting to a sustained campaign of civil resistance, in the Persian Gulf country of Bahrain begins with a 'Day of Rage'.
- 2013 – Steam for Linux is released, beginning the expansion of Valve's game service onto the free and open-source platform. This leads to 2000 games being ported to the platform in a span of a little over 3 years.
- 2015 – Two people are killed in shootings at a free-speech seminar and at a synagogue service in Copenhagen.

Births

- 1468 – Johannes Werner, German priest and mathematician (d. 1522)
- 1483 – Babur, Moghul emperor (d. 1530)
- 1545 – Lucrezia de' Medici, Duchess of Ferrara (d. 1561)
- 1602 – Francesco Cavalli, Italian composer (d. 1676)
- 1640 – Countess Palatine Anna Magdalena of Birkenfeld-Bischweiler (d. 1693)
- 1679 – Georg Friedrich Kauffmann, German organist and composer (d. 1735)
- 1692 – Pierre-Claude Nivelle de La Chaussée, French author and playwright (d. 1754)

- 1701 – Enrique Flórez, Spanish historian and author (d. 1773)
- 1763 – Jean Victor Marie Moreau, French general (d. 1813)
- 1799 – Walenty Wańkowicz, Polish painter and illustrator (d. 1842)
- 1800 – Emory Washburn, American historian, lawyer, and politician, 22nd Governor of Massachusetts (d. 1877)
- 1808 – Michael Costa, Italian-English conductor and composer (d. 1884)
- 1819 – Christopher Latham Sholes, American journalist and politician, invented the typewriter (d. 1890)
- 1824 – Winfield Scott Hancock, American general and politician (d. 1886)
- 1828 – Edmond François Valentin About, French journalist and author (d. 1885)
- 1835 – Piet Paaltjens, Dutch minister and poet (d. 1894)
- 1846 – Julian Scott, American soldier and drummer, Medal of Honor recipient (d. 1901)
- 1847 – Maria Pia of Savoy (d. 1911)
- 1847 – Anna Howard Shaw, American physician, minister, and activist (d. 1919)
- 1848 – Benjamin Baillaud, French astronomer and academic (d. 1934)
- 1855 – Frank Harris, Irish author and journalist (d. 1931)

- 1859 – George Washington Gale Ferris Jr., American engineer, inventor of the Ferris wheel (d. 1896)
- 1860 – Eugen Schiffer, German lawyer and politician, Vice-Chancellor of Germany (d. 1954)
- 1869 – Charles Thomson Rees Wilson, Scottish physicist and meteorologist, Nobel Prize laureate (d. 1959)
- 1882 – John Barrymore, American actor (d. 1942)
- 1884 – Nils Olaf Chrisander, Swedish actor and director (d. 1947)
- 1884 – Kostas Varnalis, Greek poet and playwright (d. 1974)
- 1890 – Nina Hamnett, Welsh-English painter and author (d. 1956)
- 1892 – Radola Gajda, Czech commander and politician (d. 1948)
- 1894 – Jack Benny, American actor, singer, and producer (d. 1974)
- 1895 – Wilhelm Burgdorf, German general (d. 1945)
- 1895 – Max Horkheimer, German philosopher and sociologist (d. 1973)
- 1898 – Bill Tilman, English mountaineer and explorer (d. 1977)
- 1898 – Fritz Zwicky, Swiss-American physicist and astronomer (d. 1974)
- 1903 – Stuart Erwin, American actor (d. 1967)
- 1905 – Thelma Ritter, American actress and singer (d. 1969)

- 1907 – Johnny Longden, English-American jockey and trainer (d. 2003)
- 1912 – Tibor Sekelj, Hungarian lawyer, explorer, and author (d. 1988)
- 1913 – Mel Allen, American sportscaster (d. 1996)
- 1913 – Woody Hayes, American football player and coach (d. 1987)
- 1913 – Jimmy Hoffa, American trade union leader (d. 1975)
- 1913 – James Pike, American bishop (d. 1969)
- 1916 – Marcel Bigeard, French general (d. 2010)
- 1916 – Sally Gray, English actress and singer (d. 2006)
- 1916 – Masaki Kobayashi, Japanese director and producer (d. 1996)
- 1916 – Edward Platt, American actor (d. 1974)
- 1917 – Herbert A. Hauptman, American mathematician and academic, Nobel Prize laureate (d. 2011)
- 1921 – Hugh Downs, American journalist, game show host, and producer
- 1921 – Hazel McCallion, Canadian businesswoman and politician, 3rd Mayor of Mississauga
- 1922 – Murray the K, American radio host (d. 1982)
- 1924 – Patricia Knatchbull, 2nd Countess Mountbatten of Burma
- 1927 – Lois Maxwell, Canadian-Australian model and actress (d. 1960)

- 1928 – William Allain, American soldier and politician, 58th Governor of Mississippi (d. 2013)
- 1928 – Vicente T. Blaz, American general and politician (d. 2014)
- 1929 – Vic Morrow, American actor and director (d. 1982)
- 1931 – Bernie Geoffrion, Canadian-American ice hockey player and coach (d. 2006)
- 1931 – Brian Kelly, American actor and director (d. 2005)
- 1932 – Harriet Andersson, Swedish actress
- 1932 – Alexander Kluge, German actor and director
- 1934 – Florence Henderson, American actress and singer
- 1935 – David Wilson, Baron Wilson of Tillyorn, Scottish academic and diplomat, 27th Governor of Hong Kong
- 1937 – John MacGregor, Baron MacGregor of Pulham Market, English politician, Secretary of State for Transport
- 1937 – Magic Sam, American singer and guitarist (d. 1969)
- 1939 – Blowfly, American singer-songwriter and producer (d. 2016)
- 1939 – Eugene Fama, American economist and academic, Nobel Prize laureate
- 1940 – James Maynard, American businessman, co-founded Golden Corral

- 1941 – Donna Shalala, American academic and politician, 18th United States Secretary of Health and Human Services
- 1941 – Paul Tsongas, American lawyer and politician (d. 1997)
- 1942 – Michael Bloomberg, American businessman and politician, 108th Mayor of New York City
- 1942 – Andrew Robinson, American actor and director
- 1942 – Ricardo Rodríguez, Mexican race car driver (d. 1962)
- 1943 – Eric Andersen, American singer-songwriter
- 1943 – Maceo Parker, American saxophonist (Parliament-Funkadelic, The J.B.'s, and The Horny Horns)
- 1943 – Aaron Russo, American director and producer (d. 2007)
- 1944 – Carl Bernstein, American journalist and author
- 1944 – Alan Parker, English director, producer, and screenwriter
- 1944 – Ronnie Peterson, Swedish race car driver (d. 1978)
- 1945 – Hans-Adam II, Prince of Liechtenstein
- 1945 – Rod Masterson, American lieutenant and actor (d. 2013)
- 1946 – Bernard Dowiyogo, Nauru politician, President of Nauru (d. 2003)

- 1946 – Gregory Hines, American actor, singer, and dancer (d. 2003)
- 1947 – Tim Buckley, American singer-songwriter and guitarist (d. 1975)
- 1947 – Judd Gregg, American lawyer and politician, 76th Governor of New Hampshire
- 1948 – Teller, American magician and actor
- 1948 – Kitten Natividad, Mexican-American actress and dancer
- 1948 – Pat O'Brien, American journalist and author
- 1948 – Wally Tax, Dutch singer-songwriter (The Outsiders and Tax Free) (d. 2005)
- 1950 – Roger Fisher, American guitarist and songwriter (Heart and Alias)
- 1951 – Terry Gross, American radio host and producer
- 1951 – Kevin Keegan, English footballer and manager
- 1952 – Sushma Swaraj, Indian lawyer and politician, Indian Minister of External Affairs
- 1954 – Jam Mohammad Yousaf, Pakistani politician, Chief Minister of Balochistan (d. 2013)
- 1955 – Carol Kalish, American publisher (d. 1991)
- 1956 – Howard Davis, Jr., American boxer and trainer (d. 2015)
- 1956 – Dave Dravecky, American baseball player
- 1956 – Katharina Fritsch, German sculptor and academic

- 1957 – Alan Hunter, American television host and actor
- 1957 – Soile Isokoski, Finnish soprano and actress
- 1957 – Alan Smith, English bishop
- 1958 – Francisco Javier López Peña, Spanish soldier (d. 2013)
- 1958 – Grant Thomas, Australian footballer and coach
- 1959 – Renée Fleming, American soprano and actress
- 1960 – Philip Jones, English admiral
- 1960 – Jim Kelly, American football player and businessman
- 1960 – Meg Tilly, American actress and author
- 1963 – Enrico Colantoni, Canadian actor, director, and producer
- 1963 – John Marzano, American baseball player (d. 2008)
- 1964 – Gianni Bugno, Italian cyclist and sportscaster
- 1964 – Valente Rodriguez, American actor and producer
- 1966 – Petr Svoboda, Czech ice hockey player and agent
- 1967 – Stelios Haji-Ioannou, Greek-English businessman, founded easyJet
- 1967 – Manuela Maleeva, Bulgarian-Swiss tennis player
- 1967 – Mark Rutte, Dutch businessman and politician, Prime Minister of the Netherlands

- 1968 – Jules Asner, American model and television host
- 1968 – Scott McClellan, American civil servant and author, 25th White House Press Secretary
- 1969 – Meg Hillier, English journalist and politician, Shadow Secretary of State for Energy and Climate Change
- 1970 – Giuseppe Guerini, Italian cyclist
- 1970 – Sean Hill, American ice hockey player
- 1970 – Simon Pegg, English actor, director, and producer
- 1971 – Viscera, American wrestler and actor (d. 2014)
- 1971 – Kris Aquino, Filipino talk show host, actress, and producer
- 1971 – Gheorghe Mureşan, Romanian basketball player
- 1972 – Drew Bledsoe, American football player and coach
- 1972 – Jaan Tallinn, Estonian computer programmer, co-developed Skype
- 1972 – Rob Thomas, American singer-songwriter (Matchbox Twenty and Tabitha's Secret)
- 1973 – Tyus Edney, American basketball player and coach
- 1973 – Steve McNair, American football player (d. 2009)
- 1976 – Liv Kristine, Norwegian singer-songwriter (Leaves' Eyes and Theatre of Tragedy)

- 1977 – Cadel Evans, Australian cyclist
- 1977 – Jim Jefferies, Australian comedian and actor
- 1977 – Darren Purse, English footballer
- 1977 – Elmer Symons, South African motorcycle racer (d. 2007)
- 1978 – Dwele, American singer-songwriter and producer
- 1978 – Danai Gurira, American actress and playwright
- 1978 – Richard Hamilton, American basketball player
- 1978 – Darius Songaila, Lithuanian basketball player and coach
- 1980 – Josh Senter, American screenwriter and producer
- 1980 – Michelle Ye, Hong Kong actress and producer
- 1981 – Matteo Brighi, Italian footballer
- 1981 – Randy de Puniet, French motorcycle racer
- 1981 – Brad Halsey, American baseball player (d. 2014)
- 1982 – Marián Gáborík, Slovak ice hockey player
- 1982 – John Halls, English footballer and model
- 1982 – Lenka Tvarošková, Slovak tennis player
- 1983 – Callix Crabbe, Virgin Islander baseball player
- 1983 – Rocky Elsom, Australian rugby player
- 1983 – Bacary Sagna, French footballer
- 1984 – John Prats, Filipino actor and dancer
- 1985 – Karima Adebibe, English model and actress

- 1985 – Havana Brown, Australian singer, DJ, and dancer
- 1985 – Tyler Clippard, American baseball player
- 1985 – Heart Evangelista, Filipino singer and actress
- 1985 – Philippe Senderos, Swiss footballer
- 1985 – Miki Yeung, Hong Kong singer and actress (Cookies)
- 1986 – Michael Ammermüller, German race car driver
- 1986 – Roxanne Guinoo, Filipino actress
- 1986 – Oliver Lee, English actor, director, and screenwriter
- 1986 – Gao Lin, Chinese footballer
- 1987 – Edinson Cavani, Uruguayan footballer
- 1987 – Joe Pichler, American actor
- 1987 – Tom Pyatt, Canadian ice hockey player
- 1987 – David Wheater, English footballer
- 1988 – Katie Boland, Canadian actress, producer, and screenwriter
- 1988 – Ángel Di María, Argentinian footballer
- 1988 – Siim Liivik, Estonian ice hockey player
- 1988 – Asia Nitollano, American singer and dancer (The Pussycat Dolls)
- 1989 – Néstor Calderón, Mexican footballer
- 1989 – Adam Matuszczyk, Polish footballer
- 1989 – Emma Miskew, Canadian curler
- 1989 – Brandon Sutter, Canadian ice hockey player
- 1989 – Kristian Thomas, English gymnast
- 1990 – Sefa Yılmaz, German-Turkish footballer

- 1991 – Daniela Mona Lambin, Estonian footballer
- 1991 – Chris Rowney, English footballer
- 1991 – Rilwan Waheed, Maldivian footballer
- 1992 – Christian Eriksen, Danish footballer
- 1992 – Freddie Highmore, English actor
- 1993 – Shane Harper, American singer-songwriter, guitarist, and actor

Deaths

- 869 – Saint Cyril, Greek bishop, linguist, and scholar (b. 827)
- 1229 – Rǫgnvaldr Guðrøðarson, Isles king
- 1317 – Margaret of France, Queen of England (b. 1282)
- 1400 – Richard II of England (b. 1367)
- 1440 – Dietrich, Count of Oldenburg, German noble (b.c. 1398)
- 1528 – Edzard I, Count of East Frisia, German noble (b. 1462)
- 1571 – Odet de Coligny, French cardinal (b. 1517)
- 1676 – Abraham Bosse, French engraver and illustrator (b. 1602)
- 1714 – Maria Luisa of Savoy (b. 1688)
- 1737 – Charles Talbot, 1st Baron Talbot, English lawyer and politician Lord Chancellor of Great Britain (b. 1685)
- 1744 – John Hadley, English mathematician, invented the octant (b. 1682)

- 1779 – James Cook, English captain, cartographer, and explorer (b. 1728)
- 1780 – William Blackstone, English jurist and politician (b. 1723)
- 1782 – Singu Min, Burmese king (b. 1756)
- 1808 – John Dickinson, American lawyer and politician 5th Governor of Delaware (b. 1732)
- 1831 – Vicente Guerrero, Mexican general and politician, 2nd President of Mexico (b. 1782)
- 1831 – Henry Maudslay, English engineer (b. 1771)
- 1870 – St. John Richardson Liddell, American general (b. 1815)
- 1881 – Fernando Wood, American merchant and politician, 73rd Mayor of New York City (b. 1812)
- 1884 – Alice Hathaway Lee Roosevelt, American wife of Theodore Roosevelt (b. 1861)
- 1885 – Jules Vallès, French journalist and author (b. 1832)
- 1891 – William Tecumseh Sherman, American general (b. 1820)
- 1894 – Eugène Charles Catalan, Belgian-French mathematician and academic (b. 1814)
- 1901 – Edward Stafford, Scottish-New Zealand educator and politician, 3rd Prime Minister of New Zealand (b. 1819)
- 1910 – Giovanni Passannante, Italian anarchist (b. 1849)
- 1922 – Heikki Ritavuori, Finnish lawyer and politician (b. 1880)

- 1929 – Thomas Burke, American sprinter, coach, and lawyer (b. 1875)
- 1930 – Thomas Mackenzie, Scottish-New Zealand cartographer and politician, 18th Prime Minister of New Zealand (b. 1853)
- 1942 – Adnan Saidi, Malayan lieutenant (b. 1915)
- 1943 – Dora Gerson, German actress and singer (b. 1899)
- 1943 – David Hilbert, Russian-German mathematician, physicist, and philosopher (b. 1862)
- 1948 – Mordecai Brown, American baseball player and manager (b. 1876)
- 1949 – Yusuf Salman Yusuf, Iraqi politician (b. 1901)
- 1950 – Karl Guthe Jansky, American physicist and engineer (b. 1905)
- 1952 – Maurice De Waele, Belgian cyclist (b. 1896)
- 1958 – Abdur Rab Nishtar, Pakistani politician, 2nd Governor of Punjab (b. 1899)
- 1959 – Baby Dodds, American drummer (b. 1898)
- 1967 – Sig Ruman, German-American actor (b. 1884)
- 1969 – Vito Genovese, Italian-American mob boss (b. 1897)
- 1970 – Herbert Strudwick, English cricketer and coach (b. 1880)
- 1974 – Stewie Dempster, New Zealand cricketer and coach (b. 1903)

- 1975 – Julian Huxley, English biologist and eugenicist, co-founded the World Wide Fund for Nature (b. 1887)
- 1975 – P. G. Wodehouse, English author and poet (b. 1881)
- 1979 – Adolph Dubs, American lieutenant and diplomat, United States Ambassador to Afghanistan (b. 1920)
- 1983 – Lina Radke, German runner and coach (b. 1903)
- 1986 – Edmund Rubbra, English composer and conductor (b. 1901)
- 1987 – Dmitry Kabalevsky, Russian pianist and composer (b. 1904)
- 1988 – Frederick Loewe, German-American composer (b. 1901)
- 1989 – James Bond, American ornithologist and zoologist (b. 1900)
- 1989 – Vincent Crane, English pianist (The Crazy World of Arthur Brown and Atomic Rooster) (b. 1943)
- 1991 – Vello Viisimaa, Estonian singer and actor (b. 1928)
- 1994 – Andrei Chikatilo, Ukrainian-Russian serial killer (b. 1936)
- 1994 – Christopher Lasch, American historian and critic (b. 1932)
- 1995 – Michael V. Gazzo, American actor and playwright (b. 1923)

- 1995 – U Nu, Burmese politician, 1st Prime Minister of Burma (b. 1907)
- 1996 – Bob Paisley, English footballer and manager (b. 1919)
- 1999 – John Ehrlichman, American lawyer and politician, 12th White House Counsel (b. 1925)
- 1999 – Buddy Knox, American singer-songwriter and guitarist (b. 1933)
- 2002 – Nándor Hidegkuti, Hungarian footballer and manager (b. 1922)
- 2002 – Mick Tucker, English drummer (Sweet) (b. 1947)
- 2003 – Johnny Longden, English jockey and trainer (b. 1907)
- 2004 – Marco Pantani, Italian cyclist (b. 1970)
- 2005 – Rafic Hariri, Lebanese businessman and politician, 60th Prime Minister of Lebanon (b. 1944)
- 2006 – Lynden David Hall, English singer-songwriter and producer (b. 1974)
- 2007 – Ryan Larkin, Canadian animator and director (b. 1943)
- 2007 – Gareth Morris, English flute player and educator (b. 1920)
- 2009 – Bernard Ashley, English engineer and businessman, co-founded Laura Ashley plc (b. 1926)
- 2009 – Louie Bellson, American drummer and composer (b. 1924)
- 2010 – Doug Fieger, American singer-songwriter and guitarist (The Knack and Sky) (b. 1952)

- 2010 – Dick Francis, Welsh jockey and author (b. 1920)
- 2010 – Linnart Mäll, Estonian historian, orientalist, and translator (b. 1938)
- 2011 – George Shearing, English-American pianist and composer (b. 1919)
- 2012 – Mike Bernardo, South African boxer and martial artist (b. 1969)
- 2012 – Tonmi Lillman, Finnish drummer and producer (Lordi, Sinergy, To/Die/For, and Ajattara) (b. 1973)
- 2012 – Dory Previn, American singer-songwriter (b. 1925)
- 2012 – Péter Rusorán, Hungarian swimmer, water polo player, and coach (b. 1940)
- 2013 – Glenn Boyer, American historian and author (b. 1924)
- 2013 – Ronald Dworkin, American philosopher and scholar (b. 1931)
- 2013 – T.L. Osborn, American evangelist and author (b. 1923)
- 2014 – Tom Finney, English footballer (b. 1922)
- 2014 – Jim Fregosi, American baseball player and manager (b. 1942)
- 2014 – Chris Pearson, Canadian lawyer and politician, 1st Premier of Yukon (b. 1931)
- 2014 – Mike Stepovich, American lawyer and politician, Governor of Alaska Territory (b. 1919)

- 2015 – Louis Jourdan, French-American actor and singer (b. 1921)
- 2015 – Philip Levine, American poet and academic (b. 1928)
- 2015 – Franjo Mihalić, Croatian-Serbian runner and coach (b. 1920)
- 2015 – Wim Ruska, Dutch wrestler and martial artist (b. 1940)
- 2016 – Eric Lubbock, 4th Baron Avebury, English lieutenant, engineer, and politician (b. 1928)
- 2016 – Steven Stucky, American composer and academic (b. 1949)

Holidays and observances

- Christian feast day:
  - Cyril and Methodius, patron saints of Europe (Roman Catholic Church)
  - Valentine
  - February 14 (Eastern Orthodox liturgics)
- Statehood Day (Arizona, United States)
- Statehood Day (Oregon, United States)
- Presentation of Jesus at the Temple (Armenian Apostolic Church)
- V-Day (movement) (International)
- Valentine's Day (International)
  - Singles Awareness Day

Fun February Facts

1. The birthstone for February is Amethyst.

2. Two zodiac signs for February are Aquarius (January 20 - February 18) and Pisces (February 19 - March 20)

3. The month has 29 days in leap years, when the year number is divisible by four. In common years the month has 28 days.

4. Viola (plant) and the Primrose are the birth flowers.

5. Black History Month is celebrated in Canada and United States.

6. National Day of the Sun is celebrated in Argentina.

7. In order to complete the Soviet Union's victory in Stalingrad during World War II, the last German troops surrendered in the Stalingrad pocket.

8. On February 4, 1861, a temporary committee met at Montgomery, Alabama where they organized a Confederate States of America.

9. On February 6, 1933, Amendment 20 to the United States was proclaimed which moved the Inauguration Day to January 20th.

10. In February 1910, the Boy Scouts of America was incorporated.

11. On February 6, 1899. The U.S. Senate ratified the peace treaty that led to the end of the Spanish-American War.

12. On February 6, 1952, Princess Elizabeth became Queen Elizabeth II of Great Britain.

13. February 11 - National Foundation Day in Japan

14. February 12 - Abraham Lincoln's Birthday

15. February 14 - Valentine's Day

16. February 21 - International Mother Language Day

17. February 22 - Independence Day in Saint Lucia

18. February 22 - George Washington's Birthday

19. February 24 - Flag Day of Mexico

20. February 25 - People Power Revolution (Phillippines)

www.ingramcontent.com/pod-product-compliance
Lightning Source LLC
Chambersburg PA
CBHW060445290526
45793CB00002B/580